Foundations – Faith Life Essentials
Resurrection of the Body

© 2010 Derek Prince Ministries–International
This edition DPM-UK 2020
ISBN 978-1-78263-557-4
Product Code B108D

This message is a transcript book with questions and study suggestions added by the Derek Prince Ministries editorial team.

DPM
Derek Prince Ministries
www.derekprince.com

EXPANDED
VERSION:
**GROUP
STUDY**

Resurrection
of the
Body

DPM

DEREK PRINCE MINISTRIES - UK

Contents

About This Study Series

The Bible is God's Word and our "instruction manual" to find the path to salvation in Jesus. It then shows us how to walk with Him once we have come to know Him. Logically, therefore, it is a hugely important part of our challenge as Christian believers to study the Word of God.

A sad fact is that very often we forget most of what we have heard quite quickly! As a result, what we have heard often has little impact on the way that we continue to live.

That is why we developed these Study Guides. As Derek Prince has said numerous times in his teaching, "It is a general principle of educational psychology that children remember approximately 40 percent of what they hear; 60 percent of what they hear and see and 80 percent of what they hear, see and do."

This Study Guide is intended to help you to assimilate the truths that you have heard into both your head and into your heart so that they become more than just knowledge and will begin to change the way that you live.

Living the Christian life

This study is part of a series of 10 messages, based on the doctrinal foundation of the Christian Life described in Hebrews 6:1-2 which says,

Therefore, leaving the discussion of the elementary principles of Christ, let us go on to perfection, not laying again the foundation of repentance from dead works and of faith

toward God, of the doctrine of baptisms, of laying on of hands, of resurrection of the dead, and of eternal judgment.

This mentions six specific foundation stones that we need to lay before we can build a dwelling place for the Lord in our hearts and lives:

1. Repentance from dead works
2. Faith towards God
3. The doctrine of baptisms – John's baptism, Christian baptism and baptism in the Holy Spirit
4. Laying on of hands
5. Resurrection of the dead
6. Eternal judgment.

When this teaching is applied in your life, with faith, we believe that it will deepen your relationship with God and enable you to live a truly successful Christian life.

How to Study

Each book contains a QR-code (or DVD) that links you to a talk by Derek Prince, the transcript of the talk and questions for personal application or to be discussed in a group setting.

Each video is about an hour long, divided in three parts. Set aside a reasonable length of time to read the Introduction, then watch or read Derek's teaching, and finally come back to the Study Guide to reflect on the Study Questions or to discuss them with your study group.

Once you have completed this series you will find that you have an excellent summary of the teaching. This will help you to share the content with others, whether to a friend, home group or congregation. The more you share the truths you are learning, the more they will become part of your own life and testimony.

Group Study

This study guide has been developed for use by small groups as well as by individuals.

Simply proceed through the material as a team, reflect on the questions and explore the statements together for a rich and rewarding experience.

Scripture to Memorize

In this book, we have chosen key Scriptures for memorization. They will relate in some way to your overall study. Memorizing them will place a spiritual sword in your hands which you, by the Holy Spirit, will be able to use in times of spiritual conflict.

The Word of God has supernatural power for those who will take the time and effort to "hide it in their hearts" by memorizing and meditating on it. As God's Word is hidden in your heart, it becomes constantly available to you for reference, comfort, correction and meditation. Put simply, it becomes part of your life.

Look up the verse in your own Bible and write it in the space provided. You will want to write and say this verse out loud several times until you are confident you know it well. Take time to meditate on the words and their application to your life. As a group, you could talk briefly about the meaning of the verse and its relevance to the lesson or share how you applied it.

You will be asked to recall your Memory Work at the end of the book.

Resurrection of the Body – an Introduction

This is the ninth in a series of books exploring the great foundational doctrines of the Christian faith found in Hebrews 6. Each study can serve as a stand-alone study, but you will experience an even greater blessing when you decide to do all ten studies. This study, *Resurrection of the Body*, is extremely important because they help you to live your live from an eternal perspective.

If we are objectively honest, in the world as we know it today, there's much more misery than there is happiness; there's much more strife than there is peace; there's much more sickness than there is health. Don't let us be painting a pretty picture of the world because it is not like that. You live in a fallen world, a world that has been marred through and through, corrupted and tainted by sin. That's where you are now, but thank God your final destiny as believer in Jesus is not in this world.

You know that Jesus was raised from the dead, but what does the Bible mean by this foundational doctrine of resurrection of the dead?

- What is it that gets resurrected?
- Where do Christians go when they die?
- How many resurrections are there?
- What is the significance of Jesus' resurrection, and what does it tell us about our resurrection?

Although the Bible does not reveal every detail, it does give a clear picture of what to expect from the resurrection.

Watch the Derek Prince video teaching *Resurrection of the Body* on YouTube. Scan the QR-code or visit dpmuk.org/foundations.

This video has been divided into three sections, following the chapters in this book. You will find the links to these sections when you tap the 'down arrow' to expand the information about the video.

Write down these verses and try to memorize them.

1 John 3:2

John 12:24

Since the resurrection of Jesus, the destiny of the righteous is not to go into Hades, but to a different and a much more glorious destiny.

Resurrection of the Body

In the previous book in this series, we began our study of the final two doctrines by considering the topic "At the End of Time." In that study we looked at the events leading up to the end of history and the establishment of God's permanent reign upon the earth.

Each of us, however, has a personal "end of time" that we will encounter beyond our life in this present time. For each of us, there remain two final experiences as we enter eternity. These experiences are the subjects of the final two doctrines of Hebrews 6 and the final books in this series: *Resurrection of the Body* and *Eternal Judgment*.

Beginning with this foundational doctrine, resurrection of the dead (or *Resurrection of the Body* as I have titled it), we move out of the realm of time and on into eternity. Please keep in mind that eternity does not merely consist of a very long period of time but a totally different realm of being, scarcely within the grasp of our human understanding.

First, we need to understand the meaning of the word resurrection. The Greek word, *anastasis*, means "to stand up out of." Therefore, resurrection is standing up out of death and out of the grave.

To understand what is involved in this "standing up," we begin in 1 Thessalonians 5:23–24, which refers particularly to our being ready for the coming of Jesus:

Now may the God of peace Himself sanctify you completely;
and may your whole spirit, soul, and body be preserved
blameless at the coming of our Lord Jesus Christ. He who
calls you is faithful, who also will do it.
1 Thessalonians 5:23–24

In this Scripture, we see that man consists of three elements: spirit, soul, and body. The physical body will die and be resurrected. But the spirit and the soul never need to be resurrected, because they never pass into death. Therefore, when we speak about the resurrection, we are speaking only of the resurrection of the body. To understand this, we will look at what the Bible shows us about what happens to us at death. What follows death is a matter of universal interest. It does not really matter what nationality or culture one belongs to; it seems everybody is interested in knowing what happens after they die.

What Happens after Death

In Luke 16, Jesus gives us His picture of what happens after death. I want to point out that this portion of Scripture is never called a parable. A parable is a fictional literary device used to present a truth or lesson. Jesus, however, tells this story, not as a parable, but as an event which actually happened.

There was a certain rich man who was clothed in purple and
fine linen and fared sumptuously [lived luxuriously] every day.
But there was a certain beggar named Lazarus, full of sores,
who was laid at his gate, desiring to be fed with the crumbs
which fell from the rich man's table. Moreover, the dogs came
and licked his sores. So it was that the beggar died, and was
carried by the angels to Abraham's bosom. The rich man
also died and was buried. And being in torments in Hades,
he lifted up his eyes and saw Abraham afar off and Lazarus
in his bosom. Then he cried and said, "Father Abraham, have

mercy on me, and send Lazarus that he may dip the tip of his finger in water and cool my tongue; for I am tormented in this flame." But Abraham said, "Son, remember that in your lifetime you received your good things, and likewise, Lazarus evil things; but now he is comforted and you are tormented. And besides all this, between us and you there is a great gulf fixed, so that those who want to pass from here to you cannot, nor can those from there pass to us." Then he said, "I beg you therefore, father [Abraham], that you would send him to my father's house, for I have five brothers, that he may testify to them, lest they also come to this place of torment." Abraham said to him, "They have Moses and the prophets; let them hear them." And he said, "No, father Abraham; but if one goes to them from the dead, they will repent." But he said to him, "If they do not hear Moses and the prophets, neither will they be persuaded though one rise from the dead."
Luke 16:19–31

How true Abraham's statement proved in experience! Even when Jesus rose from the dead, those who did not believe Moses and the prophets did not recognize what had happened. Sometimes we expect some tremendous supernatural visitation and think, "If that happens, I'll be convinced." But God says, "You have My Word—that is all you need. If you believe it and obey it, it will take you through." That is a very solemn thought.

There are five important truths presented in this story of the rich man and Lazarus.

First, there was persistence of personality after death. The rich man was still the rich man and Lazarus was still Lazarus. Neither of them lost their identities. Some people teach that after death everything just fades away and there is nothing left. But that is not scriptural. We continue in the same personality after death as that which we lived during life.

Second, there was recognition of persons. The rich man recognized Lazarus and Abraham, and Lazarus recognized the rich man.

Third, there was recollection of life on earth. Both the rich man and Lazarus recalled the circumstances of their lives before they died.

Fourth, there was a consciousness of their present condition. The rich man was in torment, his tongue burning with fire; Lazarus was in comfort and peace in the bosom of Abraham.

And, fifth, there was a complete separation between the righteous and the unrighteous. Each of them had an appointed place and neither could cross from one to the other.

These five features are important and they contradict a number of theories that are popular about life after death today.

1. There was persistence of personality—no loss of identity.
2. There was recognition of persons.
3. There was recollection of life on earth.
4. There was a consciousness of present conditions after death.
5. There was a complete separation between the righteous and the unrighteous.

Before the Death of Jesus

The destiny of souls before and after the resurrection of Jesus is not the same. That one event bisected human history. His death and resurrection was the most decisive event in the history of the universe and it affected what happened to those who died.

We saw in the story of the rich man and Lazarus, which was prior to the death and resurrection of Jesus, that all departing souls passed into a place called *Sheol* (in Hebrew) and *Hades* (in Greek). The word

Hades means "the unseen world."

All people alike, whether righteous or unrighteous, passed into this unseen realm called *Sheol* or *Hades*. It was a place of all departed souls, but there were two completely separate areas for the righteous and the unrighteous. Note, everybody was either righteous or unrighteous—there was no one in between. No one can be halfway righteous and halfway unrighteous. Each must end up in one or the other of those two places.

The area for the righteous was called "Abraham's bosom" meaning, I suppose, that Abraham, who is the father of all who believe, welcomed them there and comforted them. That is my understanding.

When Jesus Died

However, something profound happened when Jesus died. Jesus was a perfect man, having, as we do, a spirit, a soul, and a body. The Scripture makes a statement about what happened to each of those three elements in Jesus' personality at His death. Luke 23 speaks of Jesus' spirit:

> *When Jesus had cried out with a loud voice* [what He cried out was, "It is finished"], *He said, "Father, 'into Your hands I commit My spirit.'" Having said this, He breathed His last* [He died, expired].
> *Luke 23:46*

Jesus' spirit was committed to the Father. This is something that I cannot explain. I make this statement because it is factual, but it is a subject on which I can provide no further explanation.

What about the soul of Jesus? In Acts 2, on the Day of Pentecost, Peter quoted Psalm 16 as an experience of Jesus and not of David, who was writing the psalm. In Psalm 16:8–10, David wrote these words concerning Jesus:

> "I foresaw the Lord always before my face, for He is at my right hand, that I may not be shaken. Therefore my heart rejoiced, and my tongue was glad; moreover my flesh also will rest in hope. For You will not leave my soul in Hades, nor will You allow Your Holy One to see corruption."
> *Acts 2:25–27*

The soul of Jesus went down into the realm of departed spirits.

This is also stated in 1 Peter:

> For Christ also suffered once for sins, the just for the unjust, that He might bring us to God, being put to death in the flesh but made alive by the Spirit [or in the Spirit], *by whom also He went and preached to the spirits in prison, who formerly were disobedient, when once the Divine longsuffering waited in the days of Noah.*
> *1 Peter 3:18–20*

Jesus went down into Hades, the unseen place of the dead, and there He made a proclamation. Again, there are details of this that I cannot explain. We must simply accept what the Bible says. The New King James translation says He "preached," but the word really is "to proclaim." It does not mean necessarily that He preached the gospel, but that He made a proclamation.

My guess is He said something like: "From now on, I'm the ruler in this place. I have the keys of Death and of Hades. From now on, you are answerable to Me for everything that goes on." (See Revelation 1:18.) That is just my theory. I believe it is plausible, but it may not be right.

Meanwhile, Jesus' body was laid in the tomb. In John's gospel we read what happened to His body after He died on the cross:

> *Then they took the body of Jesus, and bound it in strips of linen with the spices, as the custom of the Jews is to bury.* [They would include a great quantity of spices because the body would be expected to decompose and give out a stench.] *Now in the place where He was crucified there was a garden, and in the garden a new tomb in which no one had yet been laid. So there they laid Jesus . . .*
> John 19:40–42

To confirm this, we can also read in John 20 the account of how the apostles and the women went to the tomb after the resurrection of Jesus. They all knew where His body had been buried, but they did not find His body where they left it. For that, we can all praise God!

From these Scriptures we can see what happened to the total personality of Jesus at His death.

- His spirit was committed to the Father.
- His soul descended into Hades, where He made a proclamation and probably did a number of other things.
- His body was laid in the tomb.

After Jesus' Resurrection

When Jesus rose from the dead, His total personality was again united. He was a complete person: spirit, soul and body. What happened through the death and resurrection of Jesus affected all of creation and also determined the destiny of souls at death from that point on. Since the resurrection of Jesus, the destiny of the righteous is not to go into Hades, but to a different and a much more glorious destiny. Here are two examples from Scripture.

When the Jews were stoning Stephen, as he was at the point of death, we read these words:

> But he [Stephen], *being full of the Holy Spirit, gazed into heaven and saw the glory of God, and Jesus standing at the right hand of God, and said, "Look! I see the heavens opened and the Son of Man standing at the right hand of God!" Then they cried out with a loud voice, stopped their ears, and ran at him with one accord; and they cast him out of the city and stoned him. And the witnesses laid down their clothes at the feet of a young man named Saul. And they stoned Stephen as he was calling on God and saying, "Lord Jesus, receive my spirit."*
> *Acts 7:55–59*

Stephen knew that his spirit was to go directly to Jesus. This is the change that has taken place because of the death and resurrection of Jesus.

> Then he [Stephen] *knelt down and cried out with a loud voice, "Lord, do not charge them with this sin." verse 60*

I believe that because Stephen prayed that prayer, Saul of Tarsus could be saved. If Stephen had not released him from his guilt, he could never have been saved. That is a wonderful and frightening thought.

I want to emphasize that if you are a true believer who has been cleansed in the blood of Jesus, living faithfully for God, the destiny of your spirit at death is to ascend directly to Jesus. Paul also refers to this in Philippians 1. He does not know which to choose, whether to continue to live here or to depart this life and be with Jesus. He says:

> For I am hard-pressed between the two, having a desire to depart and be with Christ, which is far better. Nevertheless to remain in the flesh is more needful for you.
> Philippians 1:23–24

Paul was absolutely confident that if he died at that time he would be with Christ. That is one great change effected by the death and resurrection of Jesus.

Also, at the death of Jesus the departed souls of the righteous who were in the bosom of Abraham were released into heaven. Again, I cannot fill in all the details because I do not know them since the Scripture does not provide us with further information. In Ephesians 4:8, Paul is quoting Psalm 68:18, speaking about the resurrection of Jesus:

> *Therefore, He says: "When He ascended on high, He led captivity captive, and gave gifts to men."*
> *Ephesians 4:8*

It is my understanding (and many Bible commentators agree) that the words, "He led captivity captive," mean that He released the souls of the departed righteous and took them with Him up to heaven. These righteous souls could not be released into heaven until the penalty for sin had actually been paid.

God accepted them as righteous because they had put their faith in a sacrifice that had not yet taken place. They were looking forward to the promised sacrifice. However, until that sacrifice had actually been offered—that is, the sacrifice of Jesus on the cross—they could not be released.

After Jesus had sacrificed Himself, He went down into Hades and in some way took the righteous from Hades with Him into heaven. I believe this is what the Scripture indicates. These saints had been captives of sin and death. But He took captivity captive and they became the captives of Jesus and of righteousness. This, to me, is very exciting.

MY NOTES

Study Questions

1. What special insights did you gain from this lesson?

    ----

2. Reflect on the five truths that Derek Prince derives from the story
    of the rich man and Lazarus in Luke 16:19-31. Which one was new
    to you? Compare this story to Isaiah 14:9-20. Which of these 5
    truths are reflected here?

    ----

3. What happened to all the departed souls before the death of Jesus Christ? What happened to Jesus' soul when He died? What happens to the soul of a true believer after he dies?

----

4. Why do you think God has planned for us to spend eternity with resurrected bodies rather than as spiritual beings without bodies?

----

5. Who are in Hades now?

----

6. As you meditate on Christ's resurrection, what assurance and hope can you draw from it?

----

7. Revelation 20:4-6 indicates that the resurrected righteous will reign with Christ in the Millenium. What will we be doing when we 'reign with Him'?

SUMMARY

- 1 Thessalonians 5:23-24 reveals the three parts of man: spirit, soul and body.

- It is the body that dies and it's the body that will be resurrected. The spirit and the soul never need to be resurrected because they've never passed into death. When we refer to the resurrection of the dead, it is very important to note that we are talking about the resurrection of the body.

- The story of the rich man and Lazarus recorded in Luke 16:22-26 reveals a number of things about people who have died:
  - There is a persistence of personality - there is no loss of identity.
  - There is a recognition of other people - the rich man recognised Lazarus.
  - There is a recollection of life here on earth - the rich man acknowledged Abraham's comments about his life on earth.
  - There is a consciousness of present conditions – the rich man knew what it was to be tormented in the flame.
  - There was a complete separation between the righteous and the unrighteous – neither one could cross over to the other side.

- Before Jesus' death, all souls passed into *Hades* (Greek), also called *Sheol* (Hebrew). There were two separate areas for the righteous and the unrighteous – the righteous resided in Abraham's bosom. After the death and resurrection of Jesus, the destiny of righteous believers changed so that now a believer's spirit ascends straight to God (Acts 7:59; Philippians 1:23-24).

SUMMARY

- At Jesus' death, His spirit was committed to the Father (Luke 23:46). His soul descended into Hades/Sheol (Acts 2:31; 1 Peter 3:18-19). His body was laid in the tomb (John 19:40-42). At Jesus' resurrection, His spirit and soul were reunited with His body. When He had conquered death and the grave, Jesus released the righteous from Hades and they ascended together with Him into heaven as a sheaf offering – the firstfruits of the harvest to come.

- Jesus' death and resurrection affected the whole universe – He is the firstborn from death; He is the head of a totally new creation. He is the head of a new race, the God/man race in which the nature of God and man are combined into one person.

The resurrection of Jesus is the basis for our justification. If He was not raised, we would still be in our sins. His resurrection is the guarantee of our resurrection.

Jesus' Resurrection Guarantees Ours

The resurrection of Jesus is the guarantee of our resurrection. Speaking about the resurrection of Jesus, Paul says:

> He [Jesus] *is the head of the body, the church, who is the beginning, the firstborn from the dead, that in all things He may have the preeminence* [or first place].
> *Colossians 1:18*

Jesus is the head; we believers are the body. Jesus, as the firstborn from death, is the head of a totally new creation. He is the head of a new race—the God/man race—in which the nature of God and man are combined in one person. He is the head of the body and the firstborn from the dead.

Resurrection can be compared to a birth out of death. A natural birth is such a beautiful picture of the resurrection. In a natural birth, normally, the part of the body that emerges first is the head. When the head emerges, we know for certain the rest of the body is going to follow. Likewise, the resurrection of Jesus as the head is the guarantee that His body will follow Him in resurrection.

A Pattern for Us

The resurrection of Jesus in His body is a pattern for our resurrection. Paul says in Philippians 3 that "our citizenship is in heaven" (verse 20). That truth applies to those of us who have been born again and are committed to live for Jesus. We live on this earth—we are citizens of a country here on earth—but our real citizenship is in heaven. If you are a citizen of a country, you have to have a passport from that country which is your proof of citizenship. We, too, have a passport that identifies us as citizens of heaven—the blood of Jesus.

> *For our citizenship is in heaven, from which we also eagerly wait for the Savior, the Lord Jesus Christ, who will transform our lowly body that it may be conformed to His glorious body, according to the working by which He is able even to subdue all things to Himself.*
> *Philippians 3:20–21*

Notice the mark of true Christians—that we are eagerly waiting for the Saviour.

The New King James translation of the phrase, "our lowly body," it is not a literal translation. The literal translation is very vivid: "He will transform the body of our humiliation that it may be conformed to the body of His glory."

You may not realize it, but we live in bodies of humiliation. We have been humiliated because of sin. I like to point out that no matter how wealthy or how healthy you may be, there are certain facts about the body in which you live that continually remind you that you are a sinner. You may eat the most sumptuous food and drink, but sooner or later, and generally sooner, you have to go to the toilet and empty your bladder and your bowels. No matter how wealthy you are, no matter how dignified, no matter how high your place in life, this is a body of humiliation. You may wear the finest clothes, but when you get a little bit active and begin to do something energetic, you will perspire—in more vulgar language, you will sweat. That is a body of humiliation.

God has ordained that every one of us should be continually reminded by our bodies that we are in a state of humiliation because of our sin. But, Jesus is going to change this body of humiliation into the likeness of the body of His glory. That is exciting! This body is going to change, and we will look at some of the details of the change a little later in this book.

Let me point out one very relevant fact from the first epistle of John. John says:

> Beloved, now we are children of God; and it has not yet been revealed what we shall be, but we know that when He is revealed, we shall be like Him, for we shall see Him as He is.
> 1 John 3:2

In other words, we have not yet seen the kind of body we are going to have. But when He is revealed and we see Him, our bodies will be changed into the likeness of His body.

Notice the next verse, because it is very important:

> And everyone who has this hope in Him purifies himself, just as He is pure. verse 3

John tells us that if we are truly hoping for the resurrection we will be purifying ourselves. What is the standard of purity? Jesus. "Just as He is pure..."

If someone tells me they are looking forward to the resurrection, but I see no evidence that they are seeking to make themselves more pure and more holy, I would say they are probably self-deceived. They are not really looking forward to the resurrection; they are just using religious language.

Purifying oneself is the mark of everyone who is truly looking forward to this exchange from the body of humiliation to the body of glory.

Not Limited by Time or Space

Our resurrection body will be like the body of Jesus. We observed in the record of the gospels that He was not limited by time or space. He could ascend to heaven and down again. He could enter a room with all the doors closed. He could appear in one form to one person and another form to another person. He had, shall we say, a transformable body. I believe we will have a similar kind of body.

The Pattern of Seed

People ask, "What will that body be like?" Paul deals with that question in 1 Corinthians 15:

> *But someone will say, "How are the dead raised up? And with what body do they come?" Foolish one, what you sow is not made alive unless it dies.* [Then he goes on with this example of the seed:] *And what you sow, you do not sow that body that shall be, but mere grain* [or seed]—*perhaps wheat or some other grain. But God gives it a body as He pleases, and to each seed its own body.*
> *1 Corinthians 15:35–38*

We see two truths combined here: continuity and change. If you sow an apple seed into the ground, you will not get oranges. The nature of the seed determines the nature of the life that will come out of the seed. There is continuity, but there is also change. The apple tree that comes out of the apple seed is not at all like the seed.

There will be continuity, we will be the same; but there will be a tremendous supernatural change. What is sown determines what comes up. Nevertheless, what comes up is totally different from what was sown. Our bodies are sown in burial in the ground as seeds—and the same bodies will come forth as totally different kinds of bodies. This is a vivid picture of what happens in the death and resurrection of the body.

I always marvel when I think about seeds. Think about a watermelon seed—a little black seed that you put in the ground. Who could ever believe that a gorgeous, round melon with red flesh would come up out of it? It is a continuing miracle. Every time we sow a seed, we plant a miracle—a miracle which is designed to remind us of our resurrection.

The Same Body

Jesus rose from the dead. He carefully emphasized that His body was the same body that had been crucified.

In Luke 24, we find the disciples all very frightened when Jesus first appeared to them. They could not really believe what had happened. But Jesus said to them:

> *"Why are you troubled? And why do doubts arise in your heart? Behold My hands and My feet, that it is I Myself. Handle Me and see . . ."*
> *Luke 24:38–39*

Then in John 20 there is a further record of the resurrection body of Jesus. It says:

Jesus came and stood in the midst, and said to them, "Peace be with you" [a traditional Middle Eastern greeting]. *When He had said this, He showed them His hands and His side.*
John 20:19–20

Why did Jesus do that? To show them it was the same body that they had seen crucified.

You may remember that Thomas was not there the first time Jesus appeared. So Thomas said, "I won't believe unless I can see His hands and side and put my finger into the print of the nails and my hand into His side" (verse 25). A week later Jesus appeared again and He said to Thomas:

"Reach your finger here, and look at My hands; and reach your hand here, and put it into My side." verse 27

In other words, the wound was still such that Thomas could put his hand into it. In His hands and His side, Jesus showed them the evidence of His crucifixion. He wanted to make it very plain that it was the same body, but transformed.

This is very important, because when we are resurrected, we are not going to have a new body. We are going to have the same body. But it will be changed.

Five Specific Changes

In 1 Corinthians 15 Paul tells us of five specific changes that will take place in our resurrection body:

So also is the resurrection of the dead. The body is sown in corruption, it is raised in incorruption. It is sown in dishonor, it is raised in glory. It is sown in weakness, it is raised in power.

It is sown a natural body, it is raised a spiritual body. There is a natural body, there is a spiritual body.
1 Corinthians 15:42–44

Let's take a closer look at these comparisons. The first is corruption. Corruption is decay, and anything that decays is corrupt. But when the body is raised it will be incorruptible. That is, no longer susceptible to decay.

Second, it is sown in dishonor but raised in glory. When man fell in sin, the wonderful bodies God formed for mankind became a vehicle for the sinful nature to fulfill its lusts. The bodies that were to be used to bring honor and glory to God became instead sources of shame. But, in the resurrection, the bodies which once brought us dishonor will have the glory of the resurrected body of Jesus, fulfilling the ultimate purposes for which God created mankind.

Third, our bodies are sown in weakness but will be raised in power. We may marvel at the strength of a famous athlete competing in some Olympic event. However, even those wonderfully conditioned bodies are subject to limitations and frailties. I'm not at all sure just how powerful our resurrected bodies will be. However, I believe they will not only be mighty in the physical sense, but also in the supernatural sense.

Finally, where Paul talks about a natural and a spiritual body, what he says is hard to understand. The English translations do not help very much.

The Greek word for "natural" used here is *psuchekos*, which is directly derived from the Greek word for a "soul," which is *psuche*. There is only one reasonable translation, which is "soulish." Therefore, it is better translated, "It is sown a soulish body; it is raised a spiritual body." The distinction Paul is making is between spirit and soul. In some languages (for instance, in Swedish and Danish), there is a word for "soulish." By rights, English should also have that word to correctly represent what the Bible teaches.

For instance, in 1 Corinthians 2:14, Paul writes, "The soulish man does not receive the things of the Spirit of God." But the English translations all read "the natural man" or "the carnal man." That obscures this tremendously important distinction between the soulish and the spiritual.

Thus we see that the body is sown, or buried, a soulish body; it is raised a spiritual body. I am not sure I can explain fully what that means, but I would suggest to you that in our present body the soul makes the decisions.

If I want to go through the doorway, my soul says, "We'll go through the door," and my feet obey. In a sense, our spirits are dependent upon our souls for direction. You remember that David said to his soul, "Bless the Lord, O my soul" (Psalm 103:1). In other words: "Come on, soul, get moving!" David's spirit wanted to praise the Lord, but his soul was sluggish in response.

We have to stir up our souls from our spirits to do the right thing. We know we should be praising the Lord, but our souls are sluggish and so we have to stir them up. When our body is raised, it will be a spiritual body. In other words, the spirit will control the body directly. How, I do not know.

Years ago in Denmark, where my first wife was living, there was a barber who was a rather simpleminded man. One day he said, "I had a dream. I was in a sort of body and I just pointed to where I wanted to go. If I wanted to go up, I pointed up, and I went up. If I wanted to go to the right, I pointed to the right; if I wanted to go to the left, I pointed to the left. Wherever I pointed, my body went."

I believe that is the description of a spiritual body—just a little preview of what it will be like. You will not have to work through your soul to get the body to do what you want it to do. Your spirit will make the decisions. You can accept that explanation or not; it is up to you.

A little further on in 1 Corinthians 15, Paul continues:

> ...In a moment, in the twinkling of an eye, at the last trumpet. For the trumpet will sound, and the dead will be raised incorruptible, and we shall be changed. For this corruptible must put on incorruption, and this mortal must put on immortality.
> 1 Corinthians 15:52–53

Corruptible is "that which is subject to decay"; mortal is "that which is subject to death."

If you take those two passages from 1 Corinthians 15 together, there are five specific changes that take place in our bodies.

1. From corruptible to incorruptible—subject to decay, no longer subject to decay.
2. From mortal to immortal—subject to death, no longer subject to death.
3. From dishonor to glory. A body that has been buried is a rather pitiable thing. That is how we go down to dishonor. But when we are raised, we come up with glory.
4. It is sown in weakness, but it is raised in power
5. It is sown a soulish body, but it comes forth a spiritual body.

Jesus' Resurrection Attested

Everything depends on this fact. The resurrection of Jesus is an absolutely pivotal element of Christian doctrine. We cannot set it aside and call ourselves Christians. Paul says:

> If Christ is not risen [from the dead] then our preaching is empty [vain] and your faith is also empty [vain].
> 1 Corinthians 15:14

If Christ is not risen, your faith is futile; you are still in your sins!
verse 17

In other words, the forgiveness of our sins is absolutely linked to the resurrection of Jesus. If Jesus has not been raised, the gospel is false, our faith is futile, and we are still in our sins.

There are many eminent theologians, as well as ordinary people, who have denied the reality of the resurrection of the body of Jesus. According to Paul, they are still in their sins; they are not saved.

Primary attestation: the Scriptures

Let's consider the Scripture's attestation of the resurrection of Jesus. It is an interesting fact that the primary evidence for Jesus' resurrection is not the testimony of eyewitnesses but the attestation of Scripture. Scripture takes priority over human witnesses.

First, we will consider some of the passages in the Old Testament that foretell the resurrection of Jesus. In his first epistle, Peter writes:

Of this salvation [which Peter is talking about] *the prophets*
have inquired and searched carefully, who prophesied
of the grace that would come to you, searching what, or
what manner of time, the Spirit of Christ who was in them
was indicating when He testified beforehand the sufferings
of Christ and the glories that would follow. To them it
was revealed that, not to themselves, but to us they were
ministering the things which have now been reported to you
through those who have preached the gospel to you.
1 Peter 1:10–12

The Old Testament prophets had an amazing dilemma as they prophesied about the coming of the Messiah. Peter says the Spirit of

Christ was in them, which was the Spirit of the Messiah. Under that inspiration, they spoke in the first person of things that would happen to Jesus. But they also prophesied things that never happened to themselves, personally.

Put yourself in the place of those Old Testament prophets and you will realize this must have been very difficult for them to understand. They said the most extraordinary things about themselves, but these were things that never actually happened to them. For example, Psalm 22 is known as a Messianic psalm. In other words, it is an unfolding of the revelation of the Messiah. David is speaking in the first person and he says:

> *For dogs have surrounded Me; the congregation of the wicked has enclosed Me. They pierced My hands and My feet.*
> *Psalm 22:16*

These events never happened to David! How do you think David felt when he penned those words? He was inspired by the Spirit of Christ that was in him, and he spoke in the first person of things that would happen to the Messiah but that never happened to him personally.

I have no idea how these messengers reacted to that, but it must have been quite perplexing.

Take Isaiah for another example:

> *I gave My back to those who struck Me, and My cheeks to those who plucked out the beard; I did not hide My face from shame and spitting.*
> *Isaiah 50:6*

This never happened in the life of Isaiah; but it did happen in the scourging of Jesus by the Romans. However, Isaiah wrote in the first person as if it had happened to him.

The Spirit of Messiah in these prophets, through the Holy Spirit, predicted what would happen to the Messiah, Jesus, but which never happened to them. No wonder they searched "what manner of time" they were speaking about. I marvel at the faith of these men, that they had the faith to receive these prophetic words. I thank God for their faith because it is the first confirmation of the resurrection of Christ that was predicted in the Scriptures.

In Psalm 16, which is quoted by the apostle Peter on the Day of Pentecost, we have a very amazing outline of the death and resurrection of Jesus:

> I have set the Lord always before me; because He is at my right hand I shall not be moved.
> Psalm 16:8

That verse could very well have been true of David, but it was also true of the Messiah. Frequently these messengers speak of certain things which are true in their own experience. But then they move beyond their experience into something that never actually happened to them. David goes on in verse 9:

> Therefore my heart is glad, and my glory rejoices; my flesh also will rest in hope. For You will not leave my soul in Sheol [which indicates His soul went down to Sheol], nor will You allow Your Holy One to see corruption.
> Psalm 16:9–10

David is saying, "Though I will be buried, I will have the hope of resurrection." But David goes beyond his own hope and speaks of something beyond what he could hope to experience.

In referring to the body of Jesus, he expects that it will never suffer corruption or decay. Although Jesus' body was a considerable time in the grave, because He had never committed sin, it would never see decay. Sin is the sting that admits corruption to the body. Then David says in the final verse:

> *You will show me the path of life; in Your presence is fullness of joy; at Your right hand are pleasures forevermore. verse 11*

This was fulfilled when Jesus was resurrected. He returned to the Father's presence and there was fullness of joy.

Another example is in Psalm 71, an amazing psalm. The psalmist is addressing God and he says:

> *You, who have shown me great and severe troubles, shall revive me again* [bring me back to life], *and bring me up again from the depths of the earth. You shall increase my greatness, and comfort me on every side.*
> *Psalm 71:20–21*

This never happened to any psalmist; therefore it could only apply to Jesus. He was buried; He was brought back to life; He was raised up and His greatness was increased. He became the owner of the name that is exalted above every name.

It never happened to the psalmist, but it did happen to Jesus. It was the Spirit of Messiah in those messengers testifying beforehand the things that would follow. When you begin to absorb this truth, it is the most powerful attestation of the reality of the resurrection of Jesus.

In 1 Corinthians 15:3–4, Paul said that the gospel consists of three facts: Jesus died according to the Scriptures, He was buried, and He was raised again the third day according to the Scriptures. Have you ever wondered which verse says Jesus would be raised on the third day? I have only been able to find one, and it is extremely interesting because it goes far beyond the context. It is found in Hosea:

Come, and let us return to the Lord; for He has torn, but He will heal us; He has stricken, but He will bind us up. After two days He will revive us [bring us back to life]; on the third day He will raise us up, that we may live in His sight.
Hosea 6:1–2

This is a very clear prediction of resurrection on the third day. The interesting thing is that it does not speak about "Him" in the singular, but it speaks about "us" in the plural. This is a revelation of a profound truth which was to be revealed in the New Testament.

In Ephesians 2, Paul applies this revelation. Prophecy does not merely predict future events, but it predicts them in such a way as to show their real significance. This is a perfect example written about all true believers:

But God, who is rich in mercy, because of His great love with which He loved us, even when we were dead in trespasses, made us alive together with Christ (by grace you have been saved), raised us up together, and made us sit together in the heavenly places in Christ Jesus.
Ephesians 2:4–6

God loved us even when we were dead. How many people can love a corpse? Paul here states that God has done three things, all in the past tense. Because of our identification with Jesus, we are made alive, we are resurrected, and we are enthroned. That is our destiny.

Paul does not put this in the future, but in the present, because it had been accomplished in the past. In essence, he says (if you can receive it), "You are sharing the throne with Jesus right now." This is the outworking of Hosea 6:1–2. How marvelously the Scripture interprets itself!

Secondary attestation: human witnesses

Returning to 1 Corinthians, Paul gives a list of human witnesses. This is not irrelevant, but it is secondary.

> *Christ died for our sins according to the Scriptures, and that He was buried, and that He rose again the third day according to the Scriptures, and that He was seen by Cephas [Peter], then by the twelve [apostles]. After that He was seen by over five hundred brethren at once, of whom the greater part remain to the present, but some have fallen asleep. After that He was seen by James, then by all the apostles. Then last of all He was seen by me also, as by one born out of due time.*
> *1 Corinthians 15:3–8*

This is the list of people who were eyewitnesses of the resurrection of Jesus. Most were still alive, which indicates they must have been pretty young when they saw Him. According to Jewish law, we know that the testimony of any two reliable men was sufficient to establish an event as factual. But God has given far more than two testimonies for the resurrection of Jesus.

Incidentally (and this I mention just because it interests me), Paul says he saw Jesus as "one born out of due time," or as a premature birth. I have pondered on that for a long while, but I really believe Paul was a foreshadowing of the ultimate salvation of Israel when they see the Messiah. But Paul was two thousand years in advance. He was born out of due time.

Study Questions

1. Reflect on Philippians 3:20-21. There are so many glorious truths in these verses! Before you start answering the questions below, take time to praise Jesus Christ for them.

    ----

2. Read Philippians 3:20 and compare it to 2 Peter 3:8-14. What does it mean to 'eagerly wait for the Savior'?

    ----

3. Reflect/discuss what Derek said: "According to 1 John 3:3, everyone who is looking forward to the resurrection and the second coming of Christ, will seek to make himself more pure and more holy. If he is not, he is probably self-deceived."

----

4. Why did Paul use the Old Testament Scriptures as his first authority for the doctrine of the resurrection, rather than first referring to Christ's resurrection?

----

5. Reflect on the five specific changes that will take place in your body at the resurrection. What do you think it will be like to function in a resurrected body?

----

6. How would you explain to an unbeliever or someone from a non-Christian culture (Hindu, Buddhist, etc.) the neccesity of the resurrection to the Christian faith? (See for instance 1 Corinthians 15:14, 17, 35-44; Romans 10:9)

----

7. In 1 Corinthians 15:35-38, Paul compares the resurrection to the planting of seed. Derek Prince says that every time we sow a seed, we plant a miracle which is designed to remind us of our resurrection. Consider sowing a seed or putting a flower bulb in your garden, just as a gracious reminder to this study.

----

8. What is the difference between the soulish and the spiritual life (see 1 Corinthians 2:14 and 1 Corinthians 15:42-44)? What is the

relationship between the spirit and the soul in your life now, and how will it change after your resurrection?

----

9. Read 1 Corinthians 15:14-17. According to Paul, our faith is futile if Christ is not risen. Why is His resurrection so important to the Christian faith? Why are people still in their sins if Jesus has not risen?

----

10. The primary evidence for the resurrection of Jesus is not the testimony of eyewitnesses but the attestation of Scripture. What does this imply? Read Luke 16:27-31, Matthew 28:17 and Luke 24:25-32 for your answer also.

----

11. Read Ephesians 2:4-6, 1 Peter 1:3 and 2 Corinthians 5:14-15. What does it mean to be made alive together with Christ?

The resurrection of Jesus Christ puts your life here and now in a new, divine perspective. Are you pressing toward the mark, have you got the right priorities in your life? Is the Holy Spirit pressing you to repent of the way that you have been living? If you feel you need to make changes, take time to pray about it now. Below is what Derek prayed at the end of the message, but personalized, to help you in your prayer.

PRAYER

Lord Jesus Christ, you are the author of our salvation. You are the firstfruits that rose from the dead. You are in heaven as our intercessor, You are at the right hand of the Father making intercession for me now. Because You live, I shall live also.

Lord, You see me. I have come to realize that I am not living the way I should be living in the light of Your soon Coming. God, will You pour out Your Spirit on me now in the Name of Jesus? Will You pour out a spirit of grace and supplications that I will be able to cry to You from my heart, Lord, that I will offer You sincere, humble, God-fearing prayer. Release that spirit upon me now in the Name of Jesus. Release a spirit of intercession. Oh God, have mercy, Lord.

Continue praying until you have prayed all that is in your heart. If the Lord reveals anything that is out of line with His will, repent and ask Him to show you the way forward.

SUMMARY

- The Scripture likens resurrection to a birth (Colossians 1:18):
  - Jesus is the first-born from the dead.
  - Jesus is the head.
  - The body is the Church – all true believers.
  - As with a natural birth, when the head is born, the body will follow.

- For those of us who have been born again and have committed to live for Jesus - we live on earth and are citizens of an earthly country but our real citizenship is in heaven.

- Jesus' resurrection body is a pattern for our resurrection bodies (Phil 3:20-21):
  - Our body of humiliation will become a glorious body.
  - We will be changed to the likeness of His body.
  - Everyone who has this hope of following Jesus in His resurrection purifies himself (1 John 3:2-3).
  - His resurrection body is not limited by time or space.

- In 1 Corinthians 15:35-38, we learn about the pattern of the seed and the fruit where there is both continuity and change:
  - At death, our body is planted like a seed.
  - There is continuity – what is raised up relates directly to what is sown.
  - There is also a change – planting an apple seed produces an apple tree, but the seed and the tree are very different.

SUMMARY

- Jesus identified His body as the same body that was crucified (Luke 24:38-39; John 20:20).

- There are five specific changes which take place to our mortal bodies at resurrection (1 Corinthians 15:42-44, 52-55).

	Mortal Body	Resurrection Body
i.	Corruptible (subject to decay)	Incorruptible
ii.	Mortal (subject to death)	Immortal
iii.	Dishonor	Glory
iv.	Weakness	Power
v.	Natural	Spiritual (as opposed to soulish)

- 1 Corinthians 15:14 says, "And if Christ is not risen, then our preaching is empty and your faith is also empty."

Ultimately, our destination is not heaven. Salvation is not complete until the resurrection of our body takes place.

Importance of the Resurrection

We cannot overstate the importance of the resurrection of Jesus. It is the decisive fact in the history of the universe. The whole history of the universe—not just the human race—revolves around the fact of the resurrection of Jesus.

God's vindication of Jesus

First of all, the resurrection was God's vindication of Jesus. Two courts had condemned Him to death—a secular Roman court and a religious Jewish court. When Jesus was buried, He was under that condemnation. But when He rose, God vindicated His Son. This is expressed in Romans:

> *Concerning His Son Jesus Christ our Lord, who was born of the seed of David according to the flesh, and declared to be the Son of God with power according to the Spirit of holiness, by the resurrection of the dead.*
> *Romans 1:3–4*

The Jewish phrase "the Spirit of holiness" is another way of saying "the Holy Spirit." Some translators do not realize that Paul was writing in Greek but thinking in Hebrew.

When Jesus came forth out of the tomb, God said, "I have reversed those two unjust decisions. I have vindicated My Son. He never sinned.

There is no cause for death in Him, and by My Holy Spirit I have raised Him up."

It is interesting to note that all the vital events of redemption involve all three persons of the Godhead.

The conception of Jesus was by the Father, through the Spirit, to bring forth the Son (Luke 1:35).

Of the ministry of Jesus, Peter says, "God [the Father] anointed Jesus of Nazareth with the Holy Spirit and with power" (Acts 10:38). The Father anointed the Son with the Spirit.

Of the death of Jesus, Hebrews says, "Christ . . . through the eternal Spirit offered Himself . . . to God" (Hebrews 9:14). The Son through the Spirit offered Himself to the Father.

Of the resurrection of Jesus, the Scripture says that the Father by the Spirit raised the Son (Romans 8:11; Galatians 1:1).

Finally, a statement from the Day of Pentecost: Jesus received from the Father the gift of the Holy Spirit and poured it out on His disciples (Acts 2:33).

The triunity of the Godhead is totally involved in every major stage of redemption. If I may state it reverently, it was as if no one of the persons of the Godhead wanted to be left out in this glorious visitation to the human race.

God is much more interested in us than we realize. To me, that speaks volumes. The whole Godhead was totally involved in every major phase of the process of redemption.

The basis for our justification

The resurrection of Jesus is the basis for our justification. If He was not raised, we would still be in our sins. Paul says:

> Jesus . . . was delivered up [to death] *because of our offenses,
> and was raised because of our justification.*
> Romans 4:25

Again, if Jesus had not been raised, we could not be justified. We would still be in our sins.

Then Paul says about salvation:

> *If you confess with your mouth the Lord Jesus* [or Jesus as
> Lord] *and believe in your heart that God has raised Him from
> the dead, you will be saved. For with the heart one believes
> unto righteousness, and with the mouth confession is made
> unto salvation.*
> Romans 10:9–10

It is clear that if an individual does not believe that God raised Jesus from the dead, he or she cannot be saved. It is essential for salvation.

Unfortunately, there are multitudes of professing Christians who do not believe in the physical resurrection. None of them can know the peace and joy of sins forgiven—no matter what position they may occupy in a church.

The guarantee of Christ's power to save

The resurrection is also the guarantee of Christ's power to save us.

Therefore He is also able to save to the uttermost those who come to God through Him [Jesus], since He always lives to make intercession for them.
Hebrews 7:25

If Jesus were still in the tomb, how could He save us? But because He is at the right hand of God, because He has atoned for our sins, because all authority in heaven and earth has been given to Him, He is able to save us "to the uttermost."

I love the phrase somebody once used: "From the guttermost to the uttermost." There is no limit to the power of Jesus to save. He has all power.

The completion of redemption

Then—and this is very important—the resurrection is the completion of our redemption.

Ultimately, our destination is not heaven. It is wonderful that we will be able to go to heaven, but that is just a stopping-off place. While our spirits are in heaven, our bodies will still be moldering in the grave. That is not a complete salvation.

Jesus died for the whole person, and His salvation includes spirit, soul and body. Salvation is not complete until the resurrection of the body takes place.

Paul writes in Philippians 3 that the aim and purpose of his whole life is:

That I may know Him and the power of His resurrection, and the fellowship of His sufferings, being conformed to His death, if, by any means, I may attain to the resurrection from the dead.
Philippians 3:10–11

Paul was not so concerned about getting to heaven; his ambition was to attain to the resurrection from the dead. Thank God that when we die our spirits will go to heaven. But that is not the completion of redemption, because our bodies are still unredeemed.

Paul set his sights on the resurrection by saying something very powerful: "If, by any means, I may attain to the resurrection."

He did not take it for granted that he would attain to the resurrection. We cannot assume we can just drift into the resurrection. If we are drifting, we may end somewhere else. It requires a solemn commitment and determination to attain to the resurrection.

I meet thousands of Christians who really do not take this sufficiently serious. If Paul did not assume that he would attain to the resurrection, who are we to think we will get there anyhow? Are we on the same spiritual level as Paul? Probably not. But even Paul did not take it for granted.

He said again in the next verse:

> Not that I have already attained, or am already perfected; but I press on, that I may lay hold of that for which Christ Jesus has also laid hold of me. Brethren, I do not count myself to have apprehended; but one thing I do, forgetting those things which are behind and reaching forward to those things which are ahead. I press toward the goal for the prize of the upward call of God in Christ Jesus. verses 12–14

Paul was single-minded. He said (at the time that he was speaking), "I have not arrived. I have not attained." But, he said, "There's one thing I do. I press toward the goal. I have one supreme ambition and determination—to be there when the dead are raised in Christ."

When you think of what that is going to be like, it would be a shame to miss it! It is just not possible for our limited minds to conceive the glory and the power that will be released when these weak, corruptible bodies are suddenly and gloriously transformed into a body like that of Jesus. That is wonderful to me. When I think of it, I just have to stop and ponder over it for a moment.

In Romans 8, Paul also states that salvation is not complete until the resurrection.

> For we know that the whole creation groans and labors with birth pangs together until now. Not only that, but we also who have the firstfruits of the Spirit, even we ourselves groan within ourselves, eagerly waiting for the adoption, the redemption of our body.
> Romans 8:22–23

Let me ask you a question as you read this. Is that true of you? You have the firstfruits of the Spirit. Are you groaning within yourself? Are you eagerly waiting?

What right do you or I have to suppose that God deals with us on a lesser level? The baptism in the Holy Spirit is not given to us just so we can have a good time. It is given to prepare us for what lies ahead. I feel a deep sense of solemnity about this issue.

The consummation of union

The resurrection is the consummation of our union with Jesus.

> Then we who are alive and remain shall be caught up together with them [the dead who have been raised] in the clouds to meet the Lord in the air. And thus we shall always be with the Lord.
> 1 Thessalonians 4:17

That concept is very interesting, because there are two Greek words for "air". One describes the higher, rarefied air; the other the air nearer to the earth's surface. The word that is used here is the lower air. So we will not go very far above the earth to meet the Lord.

After that, there will be no more partings. We shall always be with the Lord, and we shall always be with one another.

I had two wives (at different times!) whom I loved dearly and who both went ahead of me to glory. But one day, we will all be together forever.

Dear brother or sister, don't miss this. It is the greatest tragedy of your life if you miss this. It is earnest, and it is serious.

The Resurrection in Three Phases

Finally, the resurrection will be in three phases.

> *For as in Adam all die, even so in Christ all shall be made alive. But each one in his own order: Christ the firstfruits, afterward those who are Christ's at His coming. Then comes the end.*
> *1 Corinthians 15:22–24*

Here is the order in three separate phases: first, Christ the firstfruits; then those who are Christ's at His coming; and finally the end—the final resurrection of all the remaining dead.

For whom is Jesus coming back? "Those who are Christ's." He is not coming back for those who are not His. He is not a thief. He is not going to take anybody that does not belong to Him.

1. Christ the firstfruits. One passage from the Old Testament is very exciting in this context. This passage from Leviticus describes a ceremony under the Law of Moses.

The Lord spoke to Moses, saying, "Speak to the children of Israel, and say to them: 'When you come into the land which I give to you, and reap its harvest, then you shall bring a sheaf of the firstfruits of your harvest to the priest. He shall wave the sheaf before the Lord, to be accepted on your behalf; on the day after the Sabbath the priest shall wave it.'"
Leviticus 23:9–11

Our Saturday, as we know, is the Jewish Sabbath. The day after the Sabbath is Sunday, the day on which Jesus rose from the dead. He was the sheaf of the firstfruits, and He was waved on our behalf that we might be accepted because of Him.

But Jesus was not one single stalk; He was a sheaf. We read in Matthew 27:51–53 that when Jesus died there was an earthquake. The tombs were opened and many of the righteous dead were raised and went out into the city. They never went back into the tombs. I believe they went up with Jesus. They became "the sheaf" that was waved before the Lord, saying, "There is a great multitude to follow. Here we are; we are the sheaf. We are the firstfruits."

Jesus is the firstfruits and the guarantee of our resurrection.

2. Those who are Christ's at His coming. When Jesus returns, those who are His will be caught up to meet Him in the air and will be with Him forever. Paul writes:

For the Lord Himself will descend from heaven with a shout, with the voice of an archangel, and with the trumpet of God. And the dead in Christ will rise first. Then we who are alive and remain shall be caught up together with them in the clouds to meet the Lord in the air. And thus we shall always be with the Lord.
1 Thessalonians 4:16–17

3. Finally, the remaining dead. As described in Revelation 20, there is the judgment of the Great White Throne. This is when all the remaining dead are called forth to appear before God and answer for the lives they have lived. This, then, is the final, general resurrection. It is depicted by John the Revelator:

> Then I saw a great white throne and Him who sat on it, from whose face the earth and the heaven fled away. And there was found no place for them. And I saw the dead, small and great, standing before God, and books were opened. And another book was opened, which is the Book of Life. And the dead were judged according to their works, by the things which were written in the books. The sea gave up the dead who were in it, and Death and Hades delivered up the dead who were in them. And they were judged, each one according to his works.
> Revelation 20:11–13

I want to challenge you as you are reading this. Are you really pressing toward the mark? Do you really have the right priorities in your life?

I want to present to you an opportunity to put it right.

If you really are aware that you are not living the way you should be living, if you are not waiting eagerly for Jesus, it is time for you to change. Remember, repentance is a decision followed by an action. If repentance is needed, this is the time to do it. I have always said, "You can't repent just when you want to; you can only repent when the Holy Spirit prompts you."

You may sense the Holy Spirit telling you that you are not living right. You are not in the attitude that you should be if you are expecting His return.

If you want to put it right, I want to challenge you now and give you an opportunity to do so. I want to invite you to humble yourself and pray this prayer.

PRAYER

Lord Jesus Christ, You are the author of our salvation. You are the firstfruits that rose from the dead. You are in heaven as our intercessor. You are at the right hand of the Father making intercession for us now. Because You live, we shall live also.

Lord, I realize that I am not living the way I should be living in the light of Your soon coming. God, will You pour out Your Spirit on me now, in the name of Jesus? Will You pour out a spirit of grace and supplication that I may be able to cry to You from my heart?

Have mercy, oh God. I realize that I have had a casual attitude about the coming of Jesus and have not lived in a manner that purifies me in the expectation of His return. I give myself to You anew this day.

Remove from my heart and life those things which cloud my vision and divide my heart, so that I may look to the return of Jesus with full expectation. In Jesus' name, Amen.

May God bless you as you await the return of our Lord and Savior, Jesus Christ!

Study Questions

1. Derek Prince said about Ephesians 2, beginning at verse 4: *'But God who is rich in mercy because of His great love with which He loved us, even when we were dead in trespasses . . . He made us alive together with Christ—by grace you have been saved— raised us up together and made us sit together in the heavenly places in Christ.'* All that is in the past tense - because of our identification with Jesus we're made alive, we're resurrected and, don't stop there, we are enthroned. That is our destiny. Notice that Paul doesn't put it in the future - in essence, he says if you can receive it, you are sharing the throne with Jesus right now.'

    Write down your thoughts and turn them into a prayer.

    ----

2. Some people might argue that it is not really important whether or not Jesus physically rose from the dead. They say the symbolic meaning of His resurrection is important in itself. How would you argue with them?

----

3. In 1 Corinthians 15:3-8, Paul states that there were many eyewitnesses of the resurrected Christ. Why is it important that these witnesses were still alive at that time? What does it mean for your personal faith today?

----

4. Read Romans 4:25 and 6:23. We believe that Jesus Christ died for our sins. Why then is it important that God the Father raised Jesus from the dead? (See also Hebrews 2:9, 10:12, 1 Corinthians 15:37 and 2 Corinthians 5:15).

----

5. If you met a Christian who doesn't believe in the physical resurrection of Jesus Christ, what would you say to him or her?

----

6. Discuss/reflect: 'Paul was not so concerned about getting to heaven; his ambition was to attain to the resurrection of the body.'

----

7. The resurrection will take place in 3 stages. Describe them. (See 1 Corinthians 15:22-24, 1 Thessalonians 4:16-17).

----

8. What has changed in your perspective of your own life as a result of this study of the resurrection of the dead? How should the reality of Christ's resurrection affect your life?

----

9. Read Acts 5:26-32. Pray for yourself and for your brothers and sisters in Christ to be powerful witnesses of the resurrection of Jesus Christ.

Close this study by worshipping God for the wonderful miracle of the resurrection of Jesus Christ and our own resurrection because of Him.

SUMMARY

- The importance of the resurrection can't be overestimated. In particular, here are some specific reasons for its significance:
  - It demonstrates God's vindication of Jesus (Romans 1:3-4).
  - It is the basis for our justification (Romans 4:25; Romans 10:9-10).
  - It is the guarantee of Christ's power to save us (Hebrews 7:25).
  - It is the completion of our redemption – in other words, our resurrection body is the completion of our salvation (Phil 3:10-12).
  - It is the consummation of our union with Christ – 1 Thessalonians 4:17 says, "And thus we shall always be with the Lord." There will be no more partings.

- The resurrection occurs in three distinct phases. 1 Corinthians 15:22 speaks of everyone being made alive in Christ – "each one of us in his own order":
  - Christ, the firstfruits (Leviticus 23:10-11; Matthew 27:51-53).
  - Those who are Christ's at His Coming (1 Thessalonians 4:16-17; Revelation 20:4-5).
  - The final resurrection of all the remaining dead (Revelation 20:5).

In the next study, *Final Judgment*, you will examine the four major, successive scenes of judgment in eternity. Exploring the distinctive aspects of these four judgments, Derek Prince opens the Scriptures to bring forth the treasures hidden there.

*Recall and write down the verses you memorized
at the beginning of this book:*

1 John 3:2

John 12:24

About the Author

Derek Prince (1915–2003) was born in India of British parents. He was educated as a scholar of Greek and Latin at Eton College and King's College, Cambridge in England. Upon graduation he held a fellowship (equivalent to a professorship) in Ancient and Modern Philosophy at King's College. Prince also studied Hebrew, Aramaic, and modern languages at Cambridge and the Hebrew University in Jerusalem. As a student, he was a philosopher and self-proclaimed agnostic.

Bible Teacher

While in the British Medical Corps during World War II, Prince began to study the Bible as a philosophical work. Converted through a powerful encounter with Jesus Christ, he was baptized in the Holy Spirit a few days later. Out of this encounter, he formed two conclusions: first, that Jesus Christ is alive; second, that the Bible is a true, relevant, up-to-date book. These conclusions altered the whole course of his life, which he then devoted to studying and teaching the Bible as the Word of God.

Discharged from the army in Jerusalem in 1945, he married Lydia Christensen, founder of a children's home there. Upon their marriage, he immediately became father to Lydia's eight adopted daughters – six Jewish, one Palestinian Arab, and one English. Together, the family saw the rebirth of the state of Israel in 1948. In the late 1950s, they adopted another daughter while Prince was serving as principal of a teacher training college in Kenya.

In 1963, the Princes immigrated to the United States and pastored a church in Seattle. In 1973, Prince became one of the founders of Intercessors for America. His book Shaping History through Prayer and

Fasting has awakened Christians around the world to their responsibility to pray for their governments. Many consider underground translations of the book as instrumental in the fall of communist regimes in the USSR, East Germany, and Czechoslovakia.

Lydia Prince died in 1975, and Prince married Ruth Baker (a single mother to three adopted children) in 1978. He met his second wife, like his first wife, while she was serving the Lord in Jerusalem. Ruth died in December 1998 in Jerusalem, where they had lived since 1981.

Teaching, Preaching and Broadcasting

Until a few years before his own death in 2003 at the age of eighty-eight, Prince persisted in the ministry God had called him to as he traveled the world, imparting God's revealed truth, praying for the sick and afflicted, and sharing his prophetic insights into world events in the light of Scripture. Internationally recognized as a Bible scholar and spiritual patriarch, Derek Prince established a teaching ministry that spanned six continents and more than sixty years.

He is the author of more than fifty books, six hundred audio teachings, and one hundred video teachings, many of which have been translated and published in more than one hundred languages.

He pioneered teaching on such groundbreaking themes as generational curses, the biblical significance of Israel, and demonology. Prince's radio program, which began in 1979, has been translated into more than a dozen languages and continues to touch lives. Derek's main gift of explaining the Bible and its teaching in a clear and simple way has helped build a foundation of faith in millions of lives. His nondenominational, nonsectarian approach has made his teaching equally relevant and helpful to people from all racial and religious backgrounds, and his teaching is estimated to have reached more than half the globe.

DPM Worldwide Ministry

In 2002, he said, "It is my desire – and I believe the Lord's desire – that this ministry continue the work, which God began through me over sixty years ago, until Jesus returns." Derek Prince Ministries International continues to reach out to believers in over 140 countries with Derek's teaching, fulfilling the mandate to keep on "until Jesus returns." This is accomplished through the outreaches of more than thirty Derek Prince offices around the world, including primary work in Australia, Canada, China, France, Germany, the Netherlands, New Zealand, Norway, Russia, South Africa, Switzerland, the United Kingdom, and the United States.

For current information about these and other worldwide locations, visit **www.derekprince.com.**

FOUNDATIONS
faith life essentials

www.dpmuk.org/shop

This book is part of a series of 10 studies on the foundations of the Christian faith.

Order the other books to get everything you need to develop a strong, balanced, Spirit-filled life!

1. Founded on the Rock
There is only one foundation strong enough for the Christian life, and we must be sure our lives are built on Jesus Himself.

2. Authority and Power of God's Word
Both the Bible and Jesus Christ are identified as the Word of God. Learn how Jesus endorsed the authority of Scripture and how to use God's Word as a two-edged sword yourself.

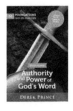

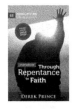

3. Through Repentance to Faith
What is faith? And how can you develop it? It starts with repentance: to change the way we think and to begin acting accordingly.

4. Faith and Works
Many Christians live in a kind of twilight - halfway between law and grace. They do not know which is which nor how to avail themselves of God's grace.

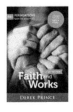

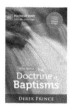

5. The Doctrine of Baptisms

A baptism is a transition - out of an old way of living into a totally new way of living. All of our being is involved. This study explains the baptism of John and the Christian (water) baptism. The baptism in the Holy Spirit is explained in 'Immersion in the Spirit'.

6. Immersion in the Spirit

Immersion can be accomplished in two ways: the swimming pool way and the Niagara Falls way. This book takes a closer look at the Niagara Falls experience, which relates to the baptism of the Holy Spirit.

7. Transmitting God's Power

Laying on of hands is one of the basic tenets of the Christian faith. By it, we may transmit God's blessing and authority and commission someone for service. Discover this Biblical doctrine!

8. At The End of Time

In this study, Derek Prince reveals the nature of eternity and outlines what lies ahead in the realm of end-time events.

9. Resurrection of the Body

The death and resurrection of Jesus produced a change in the universe. Derek explains here how the resurrection of Jesus impacted man's spirit, soul, and body.

10. Final Judgment

This book examines the four major, successive scenes of judgment in eternity. Exploring the distinctive aspects of these four judgments, Derek opens the Scriptures to bring forth treasures hidden there.

Christian Foundations Course

If you have enjoyed this study and would like to deepen your knowledge of God's Word and apply the teaching – why not enrol on Derek Prince's Christian Foundations Bible Course?

Building on the Foundations of God's Word

A detailed study of the six essential doctrines of Christianity found in Hebrews 6:1-2.

- Scripture-based curriculum
- Practical, personal application
- Systematic Scripture memorisation
- Opportunity for questions and personal feedback from course tutor
- Certificate upon completion
- Modular based syllabus
- Set your own pace
- Affordable
- Based on *Foundational Truths for Christian Living.*

For a prospectus, application form and pricing information, please visit www.dpmuk.org, call 01462 492100 or send an e-mail to enquiries@dpmuk.org

Foundational Truths For Christian Living

Develop a strong, balanced, Spirit-filled life, by discovering the foundations of faith: salvation; baptism, the Holy Spirit, laying on hands, the believers' resurrection and eternal judgment.

Its reader-friendly format includes a comprehensive index of topics and a complete index of Scripture verses used in the book.

ISBN 978-1-908594-82-2
Paperback and eBook
£ 13.99

www.dpmuk.org/shop

More best-sellers by Derek Prince

- Blessing or Curse: You can Choose
- Bought with Blood
- Life-Changing Spiritual Power
- Marriage Covenant
- Prayers & Proclamations
- Self-Study Bible Course
- Shaping History Through Prayer and Fasting
- Spiritual Warfare for the End Times
- They Shall Expel Demons
- Who is the Holy Spirit?

For more titles: www.dpmuk.org/shop

Inspired by Derek's teaching?

Help make it available to others!

If you have been inspired and blessed by this Derek Prince resource you can help make it available to a spiritually hungry believer in other countries, such as China, the Middle East, India, Africa or Russia.

Even a small gift from you will ensure that that a pastor, Bible college student or a believer elsewhere in the world receives a free copy of a Derek Prince resource in their own language.

**Donate now: www.dpmuk.org/give
or visit www.derekprince.com**

Derek Prince Ministries

DPM–Asia/Pacific
38 Hawdon Street
Sydenham
Christchurch 8023
New Zealand
T: + 64 3 366 4443
E: admin@dpm.co.nz
W: www.dpm.co.nz

DPM–Australia
15 Park Road
Seven Hills
New South Wales 2147
Australia
T: +61 2 9838 7778
E: enquiries@au.derekprince.com
W: www.derekprince.com.au

DPM–Canada
P. O. Box 8354
Halifax
Nova Scotia B3K 5M1
Canada
T: + 1 902 443 9577
E: enquiries.dpm@eastlink.ca
W: www.derekprince.org

DPM–France
B.P. 31, Route d'Oupia
34210 Olonzac
France
T: + 33 468 913872
E: info@derekprince.fr
W: www.derekprince.fr

DPM–Germany
Söldenhofstr. 10
83308 Trostberg
Germany
T: + 49 8621 64146
E: ibl@ibl-dpm.net
W: www.ibl-dpm.net

DPM-Netherlands
Nijverheidsweg 12
7005 BJ, Doetinchem
Netherlands
T: +31 251-255044
E: info@derekprince.nl
W: www.derekprince.nl

Offices Worldwide

DPM–Norway
P. O. Box 129
Lodderfjord
N-5881 Bergen
Norway
T: +47 928 39855
E: xpress@dpskandinavia.com
W: www.derekprince.no

Derek Prince Publications Pte. Ltd.
P. O. Box 2046
Robinson Road Post Office
Singapore 904046
T: + 65 6392 1812
E: dpmchina@singnet.com.sg
W: www.dpmchina.org (English)
    www.ygmweb.org (Chinese)

DPM–South Africa
P. O. Box 33367
Glenstantia
0010 Pretoria
South Africa
T: +27 12 348 9537
E: enquiries@derekprince.co.za
W: www.derekprince.co.za

DPM–Switzerland
Alpenblick 8
CH-8934 Knonau
Switzerland
T: + 41 44 768 25 06
E: dpm-ch@ibl-dpm.net
W: www.ibl-dpm.net

DPM–UK
PO Box 393
Hitchin SG5 9EU
United Kingdom
T: + 44 1462 492100
E: enquiries@dpmuk.org
W: www.dpmuk.org

DPM–USA
P. O. Box 19501
Charlotte NC 28219
USA
T: + 1 704 357 3556
E: ContactUs@derekprince.org
W: www.derekprince.org

Lightning Source UK Ltd.
Milton Keynes UK
UKHW021657130720
366461UK00005B/140

9 781782 635574